SCHIRMER'S LIBRARY
OF MUSICAL CLASSICS

Vol. 909

Peter I. Tschaikowsky

Op. 37a

The Seasons

Twelve Characteristic Pieces

For the Piano

Edited and Fingered by

LOUIS OESTERLE

✠

G. SCHIRMER, Inc.

DISTRIBUTED BY

HAL•LEONARD®
CORPORATION

7777 W. BLUEMOUND RD. P.O. BOX 13819 MILWAUKEE, WI 53213

CONTENTS

21360

January

By the Hearth

Edited and fingered by
Louis Oesterle

P. Tschaikowsky. Op. 37ª, Nº 1

Moderato semplice ma espressivo

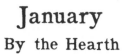

Piano

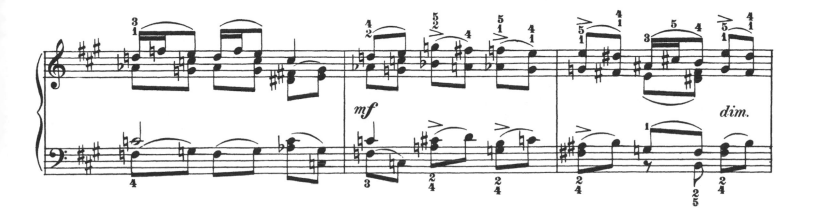

4

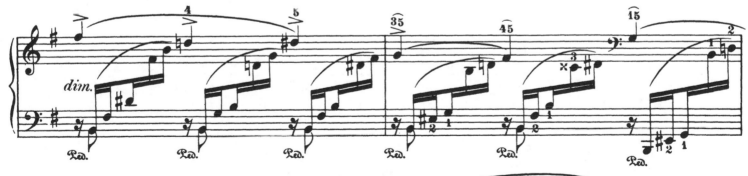

Tempo I

February

Carnival

P. Tschaikowsky. Op. 37ª, № 2

Allegro giusto

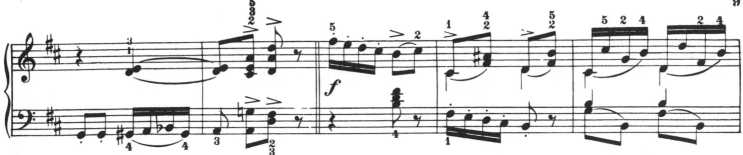

L'istesso tempo

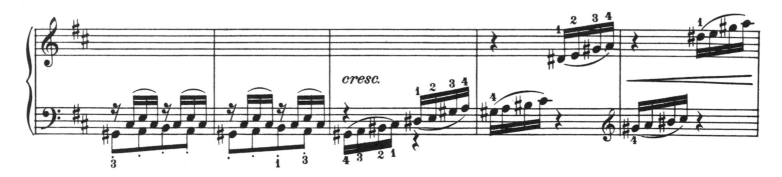

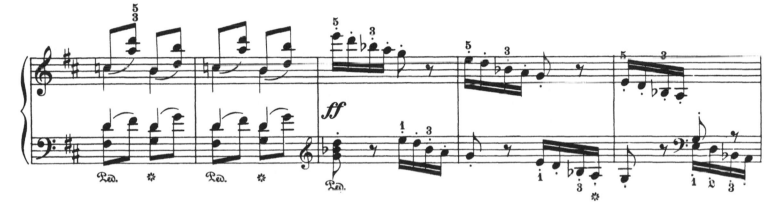

March

Song of the Lark

P. Tschaikowsky. Op. 37ª, № 3

Andantino espressivo

un pochettino più mosso

poco più f

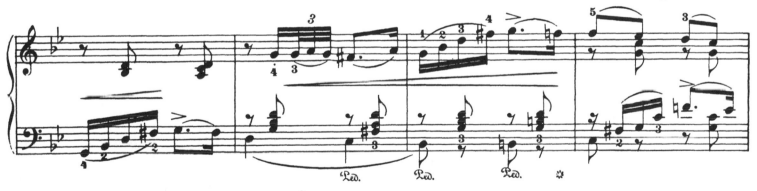

April
Snow-Bell

Edited and fingered by
Louis Oesterle

P. I. Tchaikovsky, Op. 37ª, Nº 4

Allegretto con moto, e un poco rubato

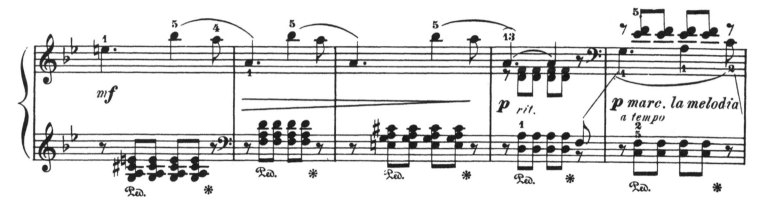

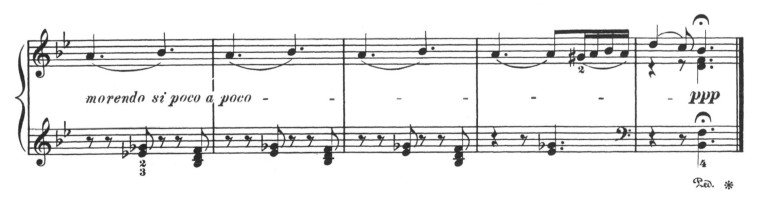

May

Starlit Night

P. Tschaikowsky. Op. 37ª, № 5

Andantino

Allegro giocoso

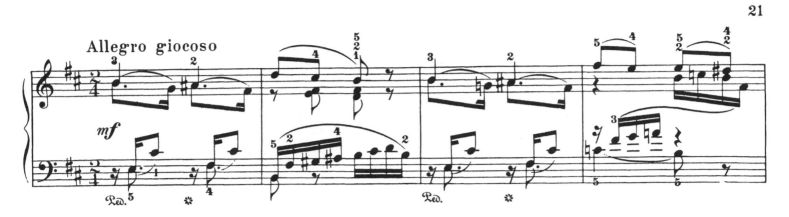

Andantino

JUNE.

BARCAROLLE.

Edited and fingered by
Wm Scharfenberg.

P. TSCHAIKOWSKY.
Op. 37, N<u>o</u> 6.

Andante cantabile.

Allegro giocoso.

Tempo I. **Andante cantabile.**

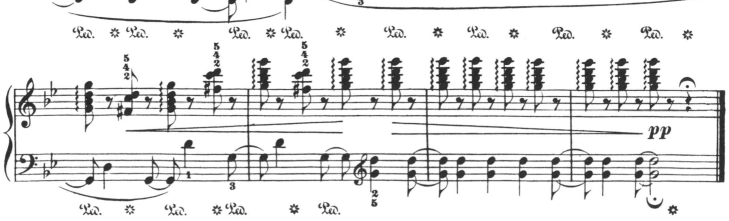

July
Song of the Reaper

P. Tschaikowsky. Op. 37ª, Nº 7

Allegro moderato con moto

August

Harvest Song

P. Tschaikowsky. Op. 37ª, № 8

Allegro vivace

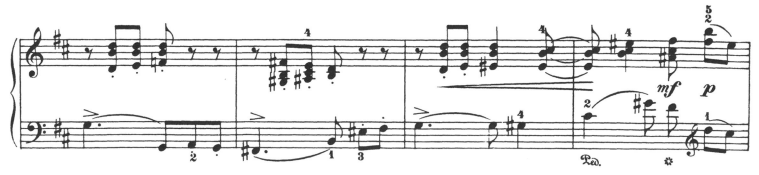

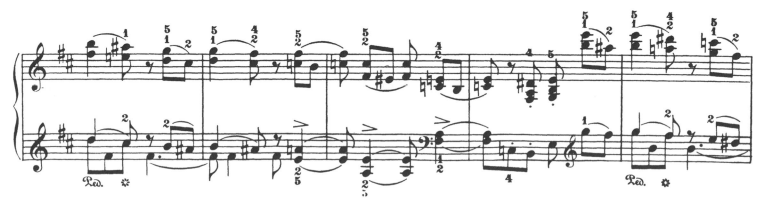

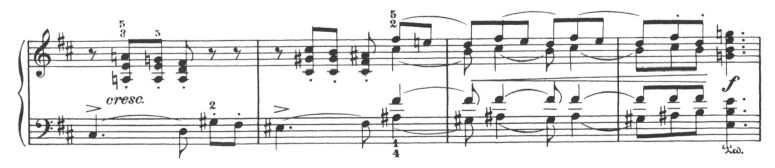

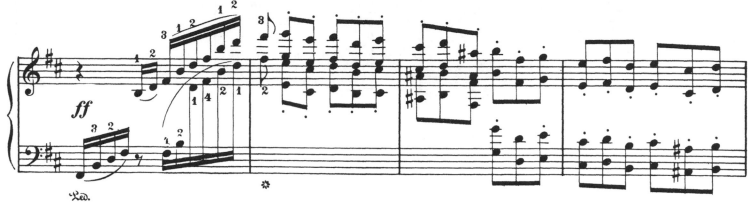

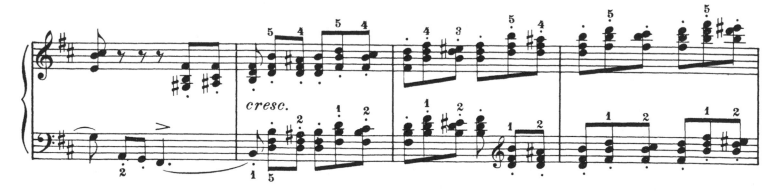

September

Hunter's Song

P. Tschaikowsky. Op. 37ª, №9

Allegro non troppo

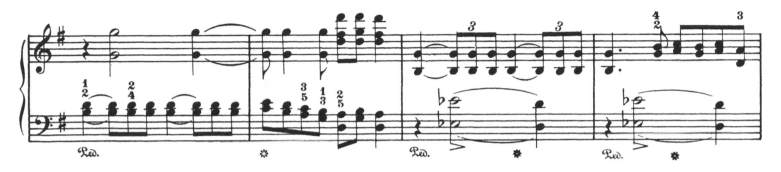

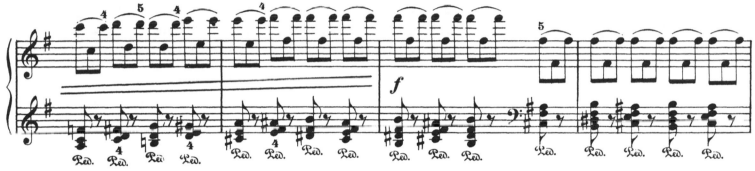

October

Autumn Song

P. Tschaikowsky. Op. 37ª, №10

Andante doloroso e molto cantabile

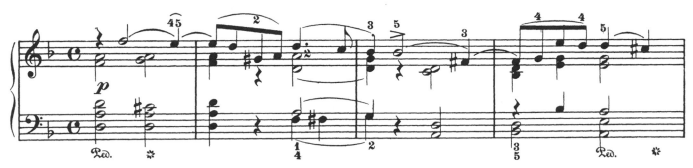

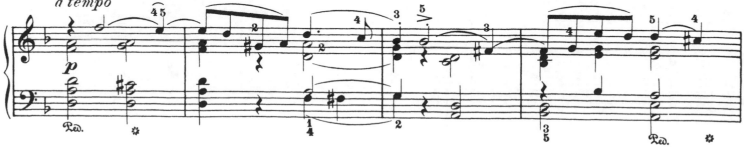

Troïka
en
Traineaux.

P. TSCHAIKOWSKY. Op. 37, № 11.

Allegro moderato.

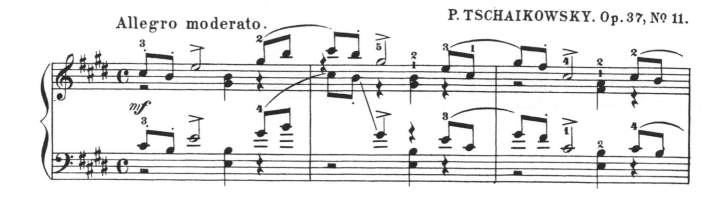

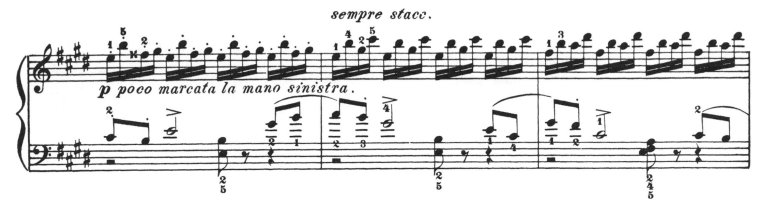

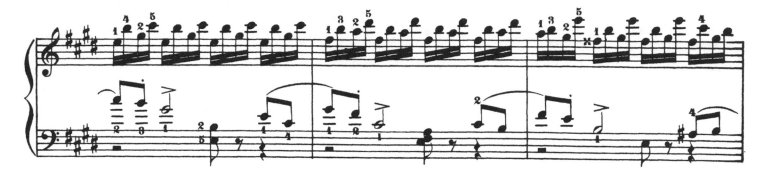

December

Christmas

P. Tschaikowsky. Op. 37ª, № 12

Tempo di Valse

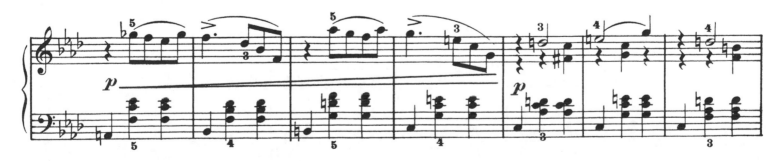

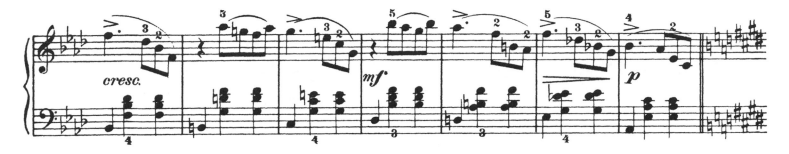

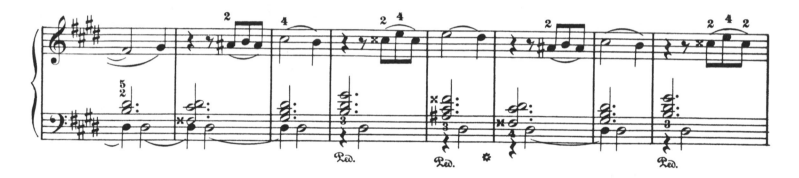

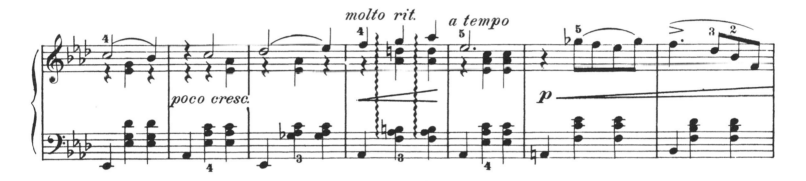

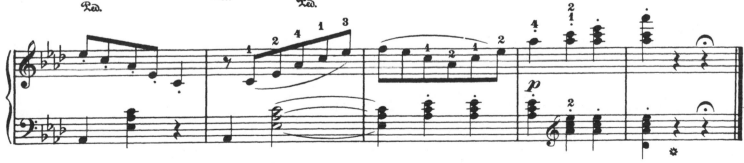